nothing more to it
than bubbles

Jane Burn

Indigo Dreams Publishing

First Edition: nothing more to it than bubbles
First published in Great Britain in 2016 by:
Indigo Dreams Publishing Ltd
24 Forest Houses
Halwill
Beaworthy
EX21 5UU
www.indigodreams.co.uk

Jane Burn has asserted her right under the Copyright, Designs
and Patents Act 1988 to be identified as the author of this work.
©2016 Jane Burn

ISBN 978-1-910834-13-8

British Library Cataloguing in Publication Data. A CIP record
for this book can be obtained from the British Library.

Designed and typeset in Palatino Linotype by Indigo Dreams.
Printed and bound in Great Britain by 4Edge Ltd
www.4edge.co.uk

Cover image by Jane Burn.

Papers used by Indigo Dreams are recyclable products made
from wood grown in sustainable forests following the guidance
of the Forest Stewardship Council.

Go to sleep, darlings, till the summer comes again.

Lewis Carroll, *Through the Looking-Glass and
What Alice Found There*

Acknowledgements

I have this theory that first published in The Linnet's Wings.
Kite, Above first published in An Anthology to Seamus Heaney,
Crow first published by The Ofi Press.
Dandelion Grasses first published by Kind of a Hurricane Press.
Driving on a Hot Day first published by Kind of a Hurricane Press.
Fairy Stories first published by Kind of a Hurricane Press.
Tea Dance Dresses first published by The Emma Press.
Harpyiai first published by Kind of a Hurricane Press.
River at Wylam first published by Material.
The sea keeps company in caves and we have breakfast at Tonia's
first published by Writers for Calais.

Also by Jane Burn

fAt aRouNd tHe MiddLe
Tongues of Fire

CONTENTS

nothing more to it
than bubbles

I have this theory that

there are invisible balls of grief
that we share among us –
the size of boiled eggs, very similar
to swallow. Enough
to stretch your throat but not
block it – leave pain after,
like you ate something that was too big
for your gullet. They don't sink
to your stomach – they lodge in your sternum
as if they are stones under mattresses –
you feel them when you bend, when you breathe,
when you walk around. Eventually,
they dissolve, are passed out
as uncomfortable dreams
when you fall asleep on the sofa.
They reform; float off, find another victim.
But they do return, as homing pigeons do.
Or salmon, swimming back
to where they were born.

The World of the Moon

Listen! Lean over the windowsill, just far enough
to feel dangerous. Just enough for the sill to press
into your chest. Ears can tune to pin-drops, lock
onto a moan a dozen streets away. *I am the sounds
of night*, I eavesdrop on a duller world, unlit save
for my muted beam. On moors, the quail speckled

to the ground like stones – the whisper of them
soughing up feathers for warmth. On luciferin seas
I hear the clear, crisp knifing of whale backs –
the phosphorescent fizz of plankton blankets broken
by their crowning spines. On roadsides – the faintest
scratch of rabbit claw, burrowing in pockled verges.

Hear the wind – silt your ears with the sound
of human shout, of traffic buzz, of hoot and squawk.
The cry of someone's baby, somewhere, needing milk.
Your ossicles will thrill to the finely distilled noises
of the dark – *all this dusk, it is mine and while
you stare out with me, it is yours.*

When Stars are Above You

You are not dead. It's only when
you're up among the them, flying
side by side, glowering upon the ridge tiles
of houses that you think *oh. So this is it?*
You may have expected pain –
have no fear. You will not remember the manner
of your death. The stars have a way of wiping
your mind clean of hurts. You will only be
aware of little things – new growth
of weed at the base of a lamppost,
the cocked eye of an owl. Every bad turn
done to you will be forgotten.
Instead, you will notice the twist
of an arctic seal, the sideways nod
of an elephants head, listening
for the crick of peanuts.
Hold out for age. For your face to take
on the look of a collapsed lung.
Try to get as far from the cradle
as you can.

This is Memory

Stitches wound patiently round hexagon edges, bound
by the needles nipped precision. She must have sat,
measuring the hours in geometric bliss, an obsession
of pinning. The delicate balancing of pinned length
on soft thigh – an occasional sharp stab in her flesh.
This pain is payment. Things of such beauty are earned.

Templates, peppered with prick holes litter her basket,
lie at her feet like paper snow. Following the direction
of the grain, fingering nap – generations have touched it
threadbare. Curious palms, cry-wet cheeks, the writhe
of naked skin on keepsake pieces. Lucky quilt,
an island of technicolour on bedsteads, soft on iron.

A floating spinnaker of flowers shaken out and settling,
fresh as washday linen, the scent of outside carried in.
Seams pressed to the width of her thumb, basted, bound
on the bias, smelling of age – all homespun dust aged
to fading. Her thoughts, listed on un-matched squares –
onions for mother   need sugar   blue thread.

Come, the Night

Slipping gentle through the window net,
the night, taking its own sweet time.
Every moment, an increment of dark –
for now, I still have the view
of the breeze in a neighbours tree,
cosseting its white flower bunches.
Fat like globules of snow.
Come slow, but come – and welcome.
I have much to learn
from the tame declining of the day.
She does not fight.
She lets the greedy dimness have its way,
knowing tomorrow brings her undiluted light.

Come On Me

Come, hands, come on me – I have much need
of your scrubbing and pawing. My skin is too big
and too small, too full of crawling beetles and chill.
Your laying on would plug a gap for a while, at least.

I have a feeling that I know what's coming –
breathe in then out through tick and tock,
lap the scald off tea to pass the turning
of the seconds, minutes, hours, days, weeks
and months it takes to build such
a monument to nothing.

I paid for love in pearls

I paid for love in pearls from the ocean floor.
Poor little shells. I split them, stole their orbs,
offered them up to sailors. Aye, they have me
in return but ever leave me behind – they cannot
warm the cold of my skin, so soaked am I in water.
Every time they break my heart, rake my scales,
cast me back among coral and bones, I swear
I will never rise again. But then I hear scraps
of their salty talk, see their faces loom above
the ceiling of the sea. Lips like jellyfish frills,
their kisses taste of kelp. Their words!
Unclasping my clamshell bra, pawing
my pickled breasts, I am a fascination for them.
They lie upon the length of me, press their mouths
to my gills and after, when they have lost
their useless germ inside me I am given back
to the waves. You cannot take mermaids to tea shops –
we do not know how to hold cups. Our language
is too deep for men's ears. They say they will be
in touch but here we have no phones. There is no place
for a stickleback on your streets. I see their fear
at the thought of my tail in a ballroom, of the sort
of footprint I would make in snow. One day I will learn
to deny the hulls above my head, stay on the oyster-beds,
watch them go. The shanties only last for a moment.
I wish I did not love their sweetness in my ears.

Sea Witch

She sang the marrow from me,
shantied my skin with her liar's mouth.
Eyes on mine, witchy as guttered flame she bade me
follow, follow, follow me man.
Follow me where there is deep.

Her hand was a halyard on my heart – she asked for roses,
red as sunset. I spilled them for her, my blood
on the shore made flowers.
Follow, follow, follow me man.
Follow me where there is deep.

My pretty Earth-love wrote to me. *Come home*
my love, my arms are emptiness, but I am caught
in the net of a Siren's eyes.
Follow, follow, follow me man.
Follow me where there is deep.

I used to think of my sweet betrothed
when seas were calm and sound was the gentle call
of wave and creak of mast.
Follow, follow, follow me man.
Follow me where there is deep.

My harpy-bride and I we are lateens,
catching the tip of the wind. I billow on her dreams –
every kiss is a keelhaul.
Follow, follow, follow me man.
Follow me where there is deep.

Barnacled by her touch she croons me cold.
My ears are full of naught
but chant and charm now.
Follow, follow, follow me man.
Follow me where there is deep.

What We Offer To the Wash

Waves like chopped blancmange
in a cut-glass dish,
gelatine peaks and troughs,
whales in aspic.
Seagull shit on cliffs
and all the while the roll and boom
of under-surface shift. Deep –
deeper than our understanding,
deep enough to burst our bodies
as if they were gooseberries.
Cold enough to stop a heart
and drink your last gasp.
The songs of giant creatures,
the pop and suck
of tentacle cups on coral rock.
The fear of such openness,
the survival of channel swimmers
who dose themselves in fat –
the churn of toxins bled by man.
The sky knows. It sits above and sees
what we offer to the wash.

I am soap

I am soap between this coat of husks. My eye is pearl.
I wonder what it feels like in the air, away from this bubbling,
wonder what it is to have legs. To dance – case my foot in satin,
swap paralysis for cabriole. I hear tiny cries of joy – my spats,
as I deliver them unto salt. Their songs are shucking-knives.
They split me. Soon for them the ever of the oyster beds.
I cannot tell them. I see my children as cloud, filtering sun
through water. Want them to be the ones that make it.

I am soap between my coat of husks. My eye is pearl.
I pretend a smile – my shell is curled with happy grins.
I see my babies off with mother's pride, feel their goodbye
in the slipstreams of their swim, touch them as best I can.
My cilia brings the taste of them to my mouth, releases it
as pain. I am meant to be cleaning the sea, but I am fouling it
with worry. Tears are lost in such expanse of liquid.
I am soap between my coat of husks; my eye is pearl.

I have shown them nothing of other worlds –
all I understand is layers of weighted frill. *Let currents
at least carry you somewhere warm.* I dream of fins.
Try to picture myself with solid form instead of scrubbing
glume to glume with all these neighbours. Hope is grains
of sand inside a stomach – chew the edges off and work
it smooth. Swallowing gets easier. I have no bone –
I am soap between my coat of husks; my eye is pearl.

I Am The Sea

I am the bump and rub of pebbles, tumbling each other
to smoothness in burnishing swell. I knead the granite
to oospore polish, lacquer them with my wetness. Sparkle
them pretty, luring human eyes with spurts of colour.
Take them away in your pockets and palms but I will keep

the depth of their tones. Their illumination will be snuffed out
inside your dried up homes. I oil the sands, sink bare footed
waders, let them feel the level of my threat. Curl them
in lather, finger paddling legs with petiole drifts. Tinge them
with fear of such headlong smashing of my face on sharp rock –

the pestle of my fists a curse called down on the barricade
of the land. I make matchwood of mighty vessels – nibble
at wrecks with appetites unsatisfied by centuries of tasting.
The tide line takes what I spit out – the blasted bones of trees,
rumbled glass, lapped by my frothy tonguing of the shore.

I have arms to love if that be my whim. Will buoy the breasts
of guillemots on my tender meniscus, sway the otter to sleep,
pads folded in prayer across its chest. I can render you driftwood.
What is sunk under the fathoms is mine to keep. I will burst
your lungs, O careless man, if you underestimate my depths.

Dead Zone

Something is sucking away our soup. Our swirls
of floatment gone, our bloom of greenling.
We only have days, must make a lifetime quick,
must sit a carpet of sheen. Make our missing selves,
shrug our spores, our little dotted babies, turn
to fragments, fuse. Make love, loose our zygotes.
We are marvellous monsters, vortex sheets
of miniature magic, tiny protist cabbages,
algae swimlings – we are the beginning of life.
Everything eats something that ate us. Sun-gobblers,
we sup on rays, dine on light. Turn our meals
to emerald stew. Inhale and suck what has been
breathed by us – we are your air. We made it
from sky and gas. Our mouths make canker-cups
but spit up pureness lip to lip for you – this
is as close as we can ever get to kissing. You pay us
in nitrogen. Sluice the fields, spray your chemical maul,
stand proud upon your swollen crop, your patch
of neighbourhood envy – lawns a chartreuse lush.
Golf on swathes of baize, marvel at the contrast
of emerald grass and white ball. You pay us in sewage,
flush your leavings into our open jaws and forget,
tickle your porcelain seats with bleach, spray flowers.
We are fury – our hearts are scarlet. We bleed, surf
a red tide, pollute instead of purify. You have asked
this of us – choke and kill. We poisoned the manatees,
grazing, adipose – gentle in islands of floating hyacinth.
We poisoned the fish. They sipped our blushing death,
went belly up. Their silver slick on shores, stinking litter.
We kill the sea where we sit. Nothing matters
in hypoxic bliss. Nothing feels or lives in Dead Zones.
Nothing swims the silence. Us, under the moon.
Deaf to whale-song, blind to the cycle of life.

The sea keeps company in caves and we have breakfast at Tonia's

And no one has a right to say that no water babies exist
till they have seen no water babies existing.
The Water-Babies by Charles Kingsley.

I
Rocky in his dirty red leather hat, face like a windfall apple.
Skin baked a mahogany windburn tang, greasy denim jacket,
bag full of papers, one woolly looking thing, beard same
as Santa. Eyes crinkled cherry pips. *Everything costs*
and you buy these things yes buy ha ha ha you know you buy
ha ha lads. We smile and say, yes, yes it does, yes?
He gurns up a pair of wet gums, turns to the invisible

companion at his table. I don't know who he is talking to
but they sure seem fun – his hands are windmills, his fingers
make bird beaks, *yak-a-yak-a. Ha ha.* Fellers come in
for the rubbish, buy coffee to go. Rocky is up, karate-chopping
the air, clasping their backs, making his happy, crack-split smile.
They know him – well, it seems, what with the way they ask
him how his week has been. We cannot make out a word

he says in answer. Time to go! Time to go Rocky!
The woman who owns the café is all brisk bustle.
Goodwomangoodwomangoood.Thjahsahujshduihfiuer
hjnerlknfpoha. Hahahahahaha. See you tomorrow, Rocky.
She thumbs his retreating back. Local character.
Lives in a cave, you know. His choice, she tells
my shocked O. His choice. Cave on the beach.

II
Fires on Blast Beach
dotted in frizzled spiders, a scorched

- 21 -

spaghetti of metal. Plastic tears
of burned bottles, sooted tins.
Are they his? Are they Rocky's fires,
or just some kids? Is this
where he cooks his tea? Is it beans
from a can with a hacked lid,
is it where he keeps warm?
Stones in a ring to stop
the flames escaping.

III
You would never come here for the weather.
The sun seems to avoid dispatching its rays below
the cliff's edge, beach the shape of a scythe.
My hair is blown to tats, spits of wet in the face -
It could be rain or spray. Inclemency

is a certainty in this place, Martian landscape
seething beneath the clifftop flora. Rocky.
Does he live here because he loves the sea?
This man who can't live in a house – lived
in a tent, got evicted, lives in a cave. I realise

who he was talking to in that café. *It's me*
that keeps him company says the creature
that is the waves. *It ain't your business, lovely.*
Have a pebble. He uses the speech of merfolk –
this is why I cannot fathom his conversation.

Whatever you want to believe, ducky.
Do you sing each other to sleep? *Him is under*
my eye. I be the lullaby. We talk as we see fit.
I suck the shores of the world. Te dua, jeg elsker dig,
mahal kita. Ha eh bak. I wanted to give

him money. They said not, said he had plenty.

His choice, his choice. What's wrong with
that man, mam? Be kind, I say. Be kind –
there but for the Grace of God. *God what?*
Bring your thoughts back to the Earth.

She rewards me with a prefect gob of glass.

IV
This is the place you come to sort out Bad Things,
nurse the burst ribcage of a marriage, talk about
the state of your brain. Easier to forgive the cracks
in the face of crumbled cliffs. They still stand, still
bear the rarity of orchids above them. Bees among
the buds, shaming the sand-flies and their grovelling
on crab death and turds. Everything here is unmasked,
whittled down to its raw – no pretty to fool the eye
or mind. A brass tacks, bottom of the pit place –
it will make you honest, it will make you afraid.
Do not look for pity. The blocked tunnels are blinded
eyes, stopped mouths. The dark soup of water holds
the breast of an occasional bird. Walk so far
that the children are as small as a fingernail, walk
back and they become the size of a thumb, a hand.
Back until they are big enough to fit in the clasp
of your arms. They taste of sea. Kiss their salty heads.

V
Water Babies, floating upwards, faces lit
by stars. The moon pipes each wave's edge
with light, makes lacework, loops little fingers,
spangles over stilled thighs. The wet is where
the souls go. Just because we splash about a bit
does not make us spirits of the sea.
Mr Theyfuckingdiedtheydid will consider

their stiff hands, turn from the image
of a ruched shirt and a bared back.
Mrs Plentywheretheycomefrom tuts at her copy
of the Daily Hate. They killed themselves *on purpose.*
Mr Sendemback will tell you maybe *now*
they will learn their lesson. I saw this bloke
with EDL tattooed on his neck. There it was,

in front of my eyes on his pig-fat neck and all
I could think for the rest of the day was that
there really *are* people like this. They are right
in front of you in buffet queues. Letters wink
from the flesh roll. His cheeks the colour of bricks.
There was this baby, nappy swollen.
A girl in a pink dress. Shoes.

VI
This water that is touching my feet, right now,
has touched them, is filled with their dying breaths.
A glove, that at some point had a hand inside it.
It could be Rocky's – my walk is a trespass
on his home. I am sure I can feel his eyes.
And no one has a right to say that no water babies
exist till they have seen no water babies existing.
The distant shouts of my children sound like bells.

Byssus

This thread between us –
from his heart to mine,
less than a human hair, less
than filament. It binds me to him,
locks us as byssus locks mollusc
to rock. I see it bite him as it bites me,
hook-in-a-fish-mouth sharp. He waves
from the window of the bus – fingers, five
baby eels, emerging from their cavern
of cuffs, as if filtering for titbits.
It hurts, it hurts. He is shoaling, lost
in a skim of too-big blazers, trousers
tiding the backs of spanking shoes.
I miss you, I miss you. The top of his head
touched with gold, body a shy reed, bending
to the height of shorter kids. I wish
he would turn – I feel the pull, the pain.
He looks back as the wave of duty
carries him on. *Be light. Be the silk
that comes from the sea.* Something
so wonderful, braided from a shell's beard –
imperfect as I am, I made this child. I wind
my devotion around the spindle of his bones,
mutter a prayer to Mazu. *Bring him home to me.*
Please. When I see him, my chest is a temple
of thanks – the undertow has not claimed him,
not today. My pearl that grew from grit,
making starfish arms, hungry after a day
of clinging to a desk with limpet palms.
I shut the door on the waves of the day,
my forehead on the bubble of glass in the door,
for a moment. My love is the clasp
of a cockle husk, closing us in.

Tian Tsui

To wear its life upon my head! Fetch me
a feathered clasp, ornaments *en tremblant*
to flit my hair, as if my head is winged.
I shall nod to you amid the blossom,
blue balanced on me as a shivered bird.
Silks stitched with views of rivers – tiny
darns of eye and beak, dewy gemstones

on my back, a river catching the face
of the sun, winding about my body.
I move as water, steps a mill-pond. Each
ripple of gown, each lotus fall of foot
marks of my royalty. Catching fallen
petals on the meniscus of my breast –
wearing flight. Caging freedoms in a crown.

The Many Voices of Crows

I sat, listened to the voices of crows.
They have this whole city, beyond the four-acre –
up there, mixed in a mesh of giant's hair.

Nests plugged in tangled orbs.
Scruffy planets caught in the web of trees, balancing
against the morning sky. The high notes –

I imagine the little 'uns yawping
in juvenile choirs. *Sing up, sing out! Waark! Waark!*
Their tutor taps her conductress claw.

Rhythm, children! Baritone,
waddling the floor, drunk from picking rich seeds
from horse muck, too fat to fly. *Howww?* They thrive,

plump on the afterbirth from lambs.
Fresh blood makes 'em shiny, keeps their eyes beady.
A murder, man calls this gathering of gloat.

Caw! A sweet voice, lighter than the rest.
The poet of the group – she is as close to a fairy
as corvids get. *Pah, pah, pah, pah!* Someone

is on the warpath – scrapping
for the better bits, arguing above their babies heads,
falling out of love. Jealous things – *cak-a,*

cack-a! Koww, koww! Every bit
of branch is a better bit, every beak a brighter one
to kiss. *Ha! Ha! Ah! Ah!* The big one,

up above the rest – He Is King,
spatters his blackberry shit where he wishes
and flashes his feathers at blinking maidens.

Lets them look at the light
making circles upon them – opens his wing tips
like fingers, offers them rings.

The Birds Know

∧

They

always did.

Have looked

down on us

since

they first put feather

to flight. They saw us cut trees out

from under them – sat on the beams we raised

in our Great Halls and sang. Watched us end each other,

denting helms, bashing our brains out. Taking, taking, greedy

as hen-coop chucks banging

their beaks down on corn.

They cried as we killed

the deer – broke

their beauty

with spears,

taught our dogs to tear

the boar and bait the bear.

They know we cannot take the sky –

^

they

watch us

raise spires,

higher and

higher,

taking as much of the blue

as we can. Dividing it up as airspace, ruling

as if we were emperors of the air, poisoning it with

atom bombs, stealing the very breath. They circle – know

that we are carrion, doomed as we are to our worlds of

wanting.

The planet will crumble

under our feet – the

sea will swallow

our heads.

We will

gulp

a last look

at above

and wish

for

their

wings.

Kite, Above
After *A Kite for Abhin*, Seamus Heaney

Hovering above some hedgerow morsel,
This bird – it has settled its focus, sharp
In loose grass. The bleach blueness of the sky

Holds the feathered body in its hot grasp.
It is a kite, a rusty slash
Of keen, pinned onto the heavens

To look below. The pips and tits
Of groundling things are only there
For hawks to press their talons to.

Angels above the hunter's head,
Leucistic wings shedding tissue,
Anaemic on pious shoulders –

The whistle of their flying, sweet
Music. Seraphim looking down
On the kite looking down on us

Souls in the wisping leaf – throstle
Song in thickets. Me on my back,
In corn, looking up. The belly

Of the kite seems as soft as breath.

Crow

Crow, beaking rubbish, garbage mouthed –
tonguing at roadkill while tasting for pearls.

Crow, passing tarry bulk through portent sky,
feels the weather on her back. Waits for sun.

Crow, tatting foot-spoor on snowdrifts, dreaming
of dance – cotillions under cut-glass light.

Crow, carving out a rattletrap of notes, opens up
her throat – pipes her ambition of song.

Crow, marble-eyed and peeping, envies the doe
her lashes – blinks her baldy lids, looks for souls.

Till Death Do Us Part

They gave each other rings,
hung dainty charcoal bands
round one another's necks.
Coo'd their betrothal all summer long
outside my bedroom window.
Courted with gentle, bumping heads,
filtered each feather on manila wings.
He lifted kisses from her neck –
she ate them in the sweetness
of her blackberry beak. I watched them,
their passion playing, little buff amalgam
of heart and song, brilliant
to evensong eyes. Those lovebirds
had grown mild with adoration,
had crooned themselves to tameness.
I was sorry for the bodies on the grass.
I was sorry that a boy could want
to fill their souls with lead.
Could fire pellets into hearts
while they were singing.

Path

Boughs laden
with fatness and sway –
sweeping skirts of green,
light-greedy leaves. The wind is play,

water is babble, birds are song –
a listing sapling makes a droopy clown.

Snails coil the plush of moss, ivy on fence-posts,
trinkets of wild primrose –
clearings sheeted in shadowed damask.
Sun dapples on the back of a rock,
lichen brooches pinned to logs.

                    Wolves. The woods knew them, once.
                    Grey snarl, loll-tongue, teeth and sly,
                                threading their pelts
                    through trunks like smoke – ancient,
                                    mythical, hungry.
                        Boar. Bristle back, hog hair,
                    kill you soon as look. Ivory teeth
                    to open up a belly, spew of
                        innards, men and spears.
                                    Stags, crowned
                        with velvet bone. Steam
                            from noses, stamp
                    of iron-shod foot, curb jingle.
                        Man, killing animal.
                        Their draw of breath.

Corn

The sun is pulsing hot above us, measuring the sky
in waves of heat. We rest – my shoulder loosed
from a cap-sleeved summer blouse, already sore
from the stubble that we broke beneath our backs.
Circled in our fortress of corn, golden faces bowed
and whispering, nodding to the rhythm of the breeze;

our noses full of summer dust, the smell of pollen,
baking earth. Lazy bees haphazard in their flight.
Nectar and honey running from the space
between my thighs to sweet the soil. Soon the cut
of harvest – the ears that heard the muted joy
of coming ground to powder, baked to bread.

Driving on a Hot Day

Liquid heat sheen blisters above sizzling tarmac.
Squint-eyed against the sun, it's like my car can walk
on water – it's like driving into melted air, like finding
a rend in the sky's fabric and passing through.

Floral turpentine aftertaste from the sticky bag of sweeties
on the dash. I am breathing daisies, singing dog-rose out
along with some song on the radio. Someone is bound
to make that joke about frying eggs on pavements.

The wheels scatter bone-dry horse shit as if it was
feathered breath. The air is hot and heavy – greenhouse
vegetation. It is almost as if I am steering blind into
silver ribbons. The road is a ripple and I am afloat.

Random Bursts

Lurid miles of neon oilseed rape – its nostril-thick,
honey mead smell cloys my throat, overwhelms
the hedgerows dozing beneath this scented blanket.
Summer trees, plump with leaves offer up
their random bursts of bloom, spattering flanks
of green. Unfettered ivy spills joyously over
crumbled stone walls, contradicting the geometry
of manicured lawns. A creeper, messages sent
on semaphore leaves, ascends a telegraph pole.
Its vines strain to smother the jabbering of cables
slicing the wash of sky – lines ever seeking
their vanishing point. A duo of crows, haloes
of light sheening on hematite wings pick
at a greasy fast-food castaway. I turn, head
to work, to clumps of brick and steel, to car-jams
spewing fumes. To the places where workers bow,
prepare to slice away more pieces of their soul,
like mean slithers of underestimated cake
eked out at an overpopulated party.

Dandelion Grasses

The
evening
wind whisks through
dandelion
grasses. Whiffled clumps
defibrillate castoff
ticks from orbicular clocks.
The green-bow stems have shaken loose
their puffball toppers, nod pale tonsured
heads at the kiss train dragged behind the arse
of the petering sun. These whispered
seeds are what remains of yellow,
sun-scald faces; plush as
lion's-mane flowers. Raising
riot on fussy lawns,
un-pullable.
Rooted, delved,
pushed in
deep.

In Season

You hurt me with your tongue.
Bake me, boil me to freckles, divide my skin
with stripes of red. Leave the mark
of straps on my back.

I like you dimmer, lower in the sky.
I adore you when your lack bleeds the acid
from leaves, mutes the landscape
with tones of soil.

I wait for colours of deeper earth,
of rust, of yellowed loss of bloom.
The sleeping until the kiss of spring
breathes life to all once more.

Men Have Come and Sketched the Road

Thou must not be pocked, sayeth them as sits in charge
of such things. Someone will send
a van of men with spades and upheaval – they must
mark the road with dashes like
a facelift, circle the offending gawps in white.
Here, in the country, nature
wants her body back – moving the smother, writhing
under sticky slag of grey.
Cometh the day, when Bimmer drivers doth complain
too much of damaged alloys
and paintjobs, as they cut from their smart-stone new-builds
to city job. Cometh this
day of judgment – spray-can diagrams, hieroglyphs
naming ugly spots. Even
a cross, as if to say, *here lies holey, gappy,*
crack. The verges are lush, wild –
their ambition to meet their opposite. Roots thread,
unstoppable. These men see
open mouths as voids needing filled – here, in their hands,
tar of salvation. Levelled,
it is easier to drive over their flattened
heads. Till then, they catch falling
water, make stoups – weeping from the very heavens,
not to be wasted. Passing
jogger, *schlopp, schlopp* on the wet, dunks his feet; is blessed.
A hymn of *bad-a-bad-a*
as we drive over, fill raggy O's with rubber.
Ploughs have cut fields to ribbons,
wavy gloam light winking from the turned marl. Settling –
a sitting back of day, a
lessening of birds. Trees hold the dark. A nearby
copse is curtained off, warning
of spook and nymph – warning that human time is done
this night. The holes wait to float
the moon, bear it gladly, this wafer on their tongues.

The Death of a Tree

Bent to November's cold passions, its unfilled twigs
tap at the window. A retch of chill from winter
spumes about its roots, chokes its sturdy bole.

Its leaves are grovelled to the ground, chlorophyll
a bleed of brown – cells disintegrating into
a web of veins amid ended flowers.

Rain, unfiltered through the knuckle crack of branches
falls to the ground like needles, sharp and cold
onto the soil, already sleeping. From inside

this room I see its knitted net of bark-rough bone,
peering in through knot hole eyes, it asks
me to quit my bed, my fireside.

Come out to me, this naked ribcage sings.
Come out to me, and hold me
in the cold.

Thrum

I have my face to the ground – *thrum, thrum.*
I hear the slow churn at the Earth's crux – her stomach
of hot ore, her rhythm, bubble of inside life. *Thrum, thrum.*

My little human thing, small as a pip on the curve
of my continents! She sends me the reverberation
of crop dusters. *Why do I need to soak this venom?*

I never had a problem with bugs. Listen, dot! Listen
to the hammer of foundations, how they plug the foot
of buildings in my flesh! She tells me about the trees,

how she grew them to be spines upon her back,
like she made the hedgehog. *They pluck them from me,*
soft-thing – see how they squash my spiky pigs,

cut me with tar. Us poets love to think we know you,
font of image that you are – I bring you my madness,
my chemical world. I believe, sister, that something

in you will fix me. *Stop looking, funny fish – stop looking*
for men to be mirrors. Spend a million, million years
getting to know yourself. This giant ball was not built

overnight. Think of layers. Life is poison –
I suck it as you take the scat of man. Forty four
rings of age – our forms an onion of stories.

I am stone, have forgotten how to be organic.
Plant yourself, wombling, look to your leaves. Somewhere
is lava. Lie here and wake. Crust, mantle, core –

I am bruises, she is bruises. I could be new as spring,
I could be snowflakes. *Who can predict the weather? Smile,*
my grimmish friend – curdle bird-sing in your shell.

The deadest things grow back with the right breath.
Stop craving, lambkin and live. Peoples spraying
canned flowers over shit – be not them. I wish

I had not bred them, some days. But then, they play the harp,
put ribbons in a Clydesdale's tail and I love them again.
She wraps me in grasses. I witness the progress of clouds.

Harpyiai

I shall wear the name *harpy* as armour – it is no insult
to be Aellai. I am no gust – I hit the dirt hard, I am
a hurricane. Open my mouth and spit typhoons, snatch
up your frowns, turn them in my twists. Only a bloke
could wax such words about ugliness – as if only the kind
are beautiful, only the fair of face are allowed to be loved.
Who has sat you man, as judge of our worth? No wonder
I rattle the air in my wings – spread them, knock you flat
with backdraft, fly you a face-full of feathers. See my body –
my skin is prickle sprout, my legs were a spatchcock
as I pushed my baby out. My wild-horse child, his Anemoi dad
busy blowing the hills about, all bombast. Air is a delicate thing
if we leave it alone – just breathe, nothing more. *Your voice
is sharp,* he says. Beak ever ready to bite. He does not hear
the gentle song I give to the end of day – he does not see
my half-bird body sparrow hop round supermarkets, peck
at the washing line with pegs. I gave my heart to Boreas –
he blew a winter's chill over the landscape of our love,
lapped about our home until it was a seat of ice. Our nest
is lined with frost – we find no comfort in these frigid twigs.
I should cast him to my sisters, born of atmosphere
and Earth – Erinyes, furious at them who did not keep
their oaths. I feel them beat the ground above their heads –
send us your faithless! I cast my face to floor,
hoping to feel them, cheek on cheek. They shall not
call us crones! Not when we have been hacked and hurt –
we are shafts of survival. We are more dazzling
than those men will ever understand.

Fascinated Fairy

She plants her faun-steps into crumpled floor, feels them
slip on leaf-mould. Fay of the forest, the crack of riven twig
startling the thin of dawn air. Daal'mist for a dress, cotton
of fogged fur about her, cloaked. Legs brittle, stepping through

lacework, haze of shin swad plucking tiny clouds
to itself – the morning's drift. *Come light, come light.*
She bids it break, chase the ghosts of dark –
too many things, too many things in shade. She spent

the night in a doze of imaginings, saw visions, her mouth,
open wide as a gloup. Insides turning outside, passing
through herself time and time again. Her softly puff
of breath awakes Prince Heyghoge, wound in the grotto

of her cupped hands. *Yes, yes,* she twiddles, rapt at his jigger
of rousing spines. Offers him worms. *I shall learn the workings
of your inner tracts,* she tells him. *There shall be
no secrets within.* She was not always a wood-nymph –

once she was a creature of river and sea, fascination
for all wet things. Floating frame a causeway,
curve of water ever moiling to meet itself over her head.
Her bliss was the dance of manta, flocking the ocean,

flying the currents. Mermaid's purses, hearts of fishling
doodling somersaults inside. *Grow, grow. Let me guess
at your mystery.* She wore them, strung on chains
around her neck, wore their yolk and beating hearts

like pulsing beads. She lay in tide spit, made happy
with merfolk, fell in and out of love. Kissed salt,
sweated salt, sucked the shore dry of dreams –
lay on her back and considered sky. As waves lapped,

she wondered, *how do they fly, these birds?* She lived
for a while as a swan, a swift, a nightingale –
where every woman who was ever hurt is a Philomela,
in the pure of air. Opened her wings and span,

around and round for joy. She was a volcano's core,
keeping her hotness bubbling under crust, feelt footsteps
dawdling on her chest, heard voices loosing echoes
into the gasp of her dormant wound. *Man! The one animal*

this Earth never needed. Anger made her cough her ash
in wolfsnow clouds – when she had held her breath too long,
she let her lava out. Her face was a rindle bed, dead
without rain. *Can a body exist as a desert?* She was

a kingdom of secrets. Seeds that only bloom with flood,
flower and die, sands that shift a different pattern daily.
She thirsted for snow-melt – watched crafty ponies chew
on dalur grasses, teach themselves to tolt. Yearned

for colder yet, saw the silent loom of bergs, swam beneath
to spy their hidden halves. *How heavy, to carry*
these swallowed selves. Hands in the pelt of ice bears,
she walked the skim of jigsaw floe, flakes landing

skith on her hair. Always a metal measuring thing,
a monument, trash-pile, jumble of wires, encroachment
of brick. *The concrete wants us! One day, my hedgepig,*
there will be no room for us. You will learn snuffle

your grubs among patio furniture – will mummify at roadsides.
You will fear wheels. How I shall miss you! Both with our spikes
and need to curl. We shall reach our end in this smother
of civilisation. As trees were plucked from the planet,

she tried to be a caryatid, propping the boughs. Broke
under catastrophe, saw the discord of gulls gorging on landfill.
Mourned over sacks of dried seahorses, bagged
in compressed wisps – grains of gone-ness. She tried

- 46 -

to free them once but they only made a flotilla of sad quirks.
Go little creatures! Leave me to my contemplation of vapours.
She became oxygen, taken to the lungs of every person,
strained in and out. The exhalations bleed her bit by bit –

each sigh from them a loss of some piece of her. The hedgehog
quits her palm. She is ebbing, a half-life. He finds no comfort
in a vanishing embrace. They suck, they blow. They take
the atmosphere. She is emptied by their breaths.

Accessible Only By Boat

I am a periwinkle – ovate, curled, a screw in the sand.
Today, the air is balm. The storm of yesterday cast me,
body a marble in the might of its eye. I will have bruises.
At some point I will tentatively check, count my fingers,
dab through the roots of the hair on my head. My brain is big
against its casket of skull, swollen with thoughts, but now
 I lay it down on the peace of the shore, hear the waves
play kiss-chase, whispering, *come, go. Come, go* –
it is all the same to water. Float or sink, sup or parch –
I am nothing more to it than bubbles. I shall follow

its brackish firth when I have need and find it fresher,
pooled for my mouth, trapped in the dish of tree roots.
 Fires! I will set them, signals along the shore, tend them
night and day. All those women – all those souls who sit
like me and stare from windows, out onto quads of patched lawn,
wheelie bins, cats on fences, clothes props, car parks,
clouds. If they see the blaze I set for them, they will come
to this paradise, accessible only by boat. We will learn
the route of rain, trace its journey from sky to leaf, to puddle,
stream, river, salted estuary, sea. Let us be liquid, float

on our backs spread ourselves as if we are fallen stars,
open our throats to the air. Taste the breath of those we love –
our children are a spike in our lungs, a pain in our chests.
We set them loose to the world then live as nets, forever
waiting to catch their fall. See my signals! Throw yourselves
to the wet and let it bear you to this island – we can dance
the banshee dance, swing our tits and sagging arse cracks,
have our worst bits licked by flames in moonlight. Feel no shame
and laugh our madness, *ah-ha-ha-ha-ha-ha-ha-ha!* Here,
we do not need to press our teeth to meat. The fish can stay

as brightness in the drink – we do not want the blood

of living things. The atoll birds will light in our laps –
beak us stories of their travel, invite us to share their nests,
lend their wasted feathers so we might set them in tangled hair
and dream of flight. When the morning wakes us, calls us back
to bedside, bus route, keyboard, wash, we can recall
our wild-witch ways. Our hearts are eyeballs – they have seen
too much, have been poked in their humors too many times,
each person held inside a hordeolum. Once in a while,
we let another person cross our causeway, make our grains

sing as they sink their own weight in our slick. I will work
to cut this isthmus – be a no-man's-land, keep myself a cay,
let spray skin me to salcrete. I show the sun my cowrie grin,
 bake spread-eagled. Reach to connect with other bodies, lying
the same. I don't need to meet their faces with mine –
I know the look I will find there. Instead we hook fingers together,
ride the slow spin of the Earth, carpet the beach with a great
connection of selves. When I am plunged in suds I shall believe
I am salved in foam – car alarms are conch-calls.
Sleeves on a line are petrel's wings.

Perlemorskyer

The underside of a buzzard above
me again. This one, a curl of chocolate
dark etching the afternoon, porridge-meal
stomach against a lid of bleachy silver,
cloudless, cold. I wonder if it is wishing
for sheep as she makes these forays
over the fields – a better ambition than rats.
One I saw flew so low I saw its eye. Hovering
gardens, depth of winter driving it out
with thoughts of pet rabbits. A big one,
hieroglyph on a fence post – it does not
trouble itself to move. It shrugs my gape,
squints at the snow, spindrift on heifer backs.
The herd is balled, tight with hair and legs,
blowing at the sight of me while they wait,
growing to sirloin. Its mate, up in the air.

This magic of flight we crave – leaping
from the Eiger with plastic wings,
climbing mountains on thinning air and whizz.
I want to ask them – *did you see the lights?*
Did you go where sky is painted like pearls?